The Runaway Brain

by

Debby Livingston Green

illustrations by

Susan & Scott Sirkin

www.12photo.com

Dedicated to my son, Bradley Brunken,
and my daughter, Brittany Brunken,
who were with me one night when I
wrote this poem, and who still send me
messages to, "Go to sleep."

You've heard of a runaway bus
And a runaway train,

But have you ever imagined
A runaway brain?!

Try as you might
You can't hold it down,
It flies uncontrolled
All over the town.

It goes up the mountain
And down the hill,
Spinning and fluttering
At its own will.

It looks at the present,
It thinks about the past,
It wonders at the future,
Oh, how long will this last?!

It worries about things
Where it holds no control,
There's no rest for your heart,
Or your mind, or your soul.

It zips along its way
Unleashed and wild,
Like a head of hair
Uncombed and unstyled.

Sometimes it's exhausted
And tries to sleep,
But then a new thought
Into its cells will leap.

It can't resist.
It stands on little brain feet.
And dashes off,
A new thought to meet!

Then Zip! Zip! Zip!
And Trip! Trip! Trip!
You have to be careful
Or your mind will flip.

Sometimes happy,
And sometimes sad,
It matters not if thoughts
Are good or bad.

For it keeps you awake
Just the same,
On and on it goes
With its little game.

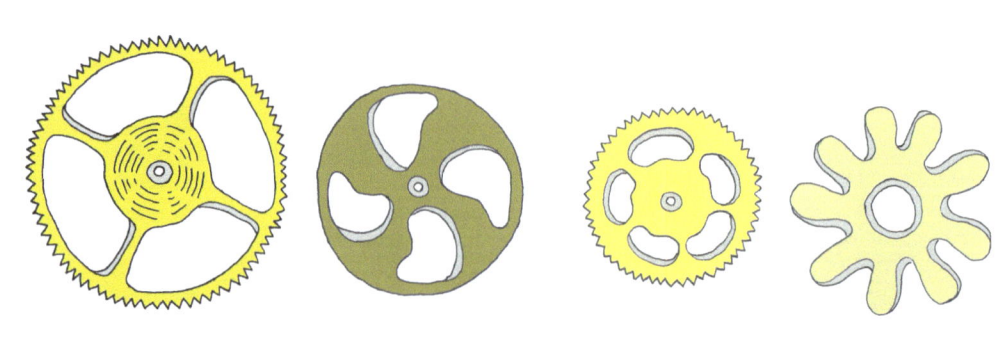

So, if you happen to have
A runaway brain,
Please try and try,
And learn to contain

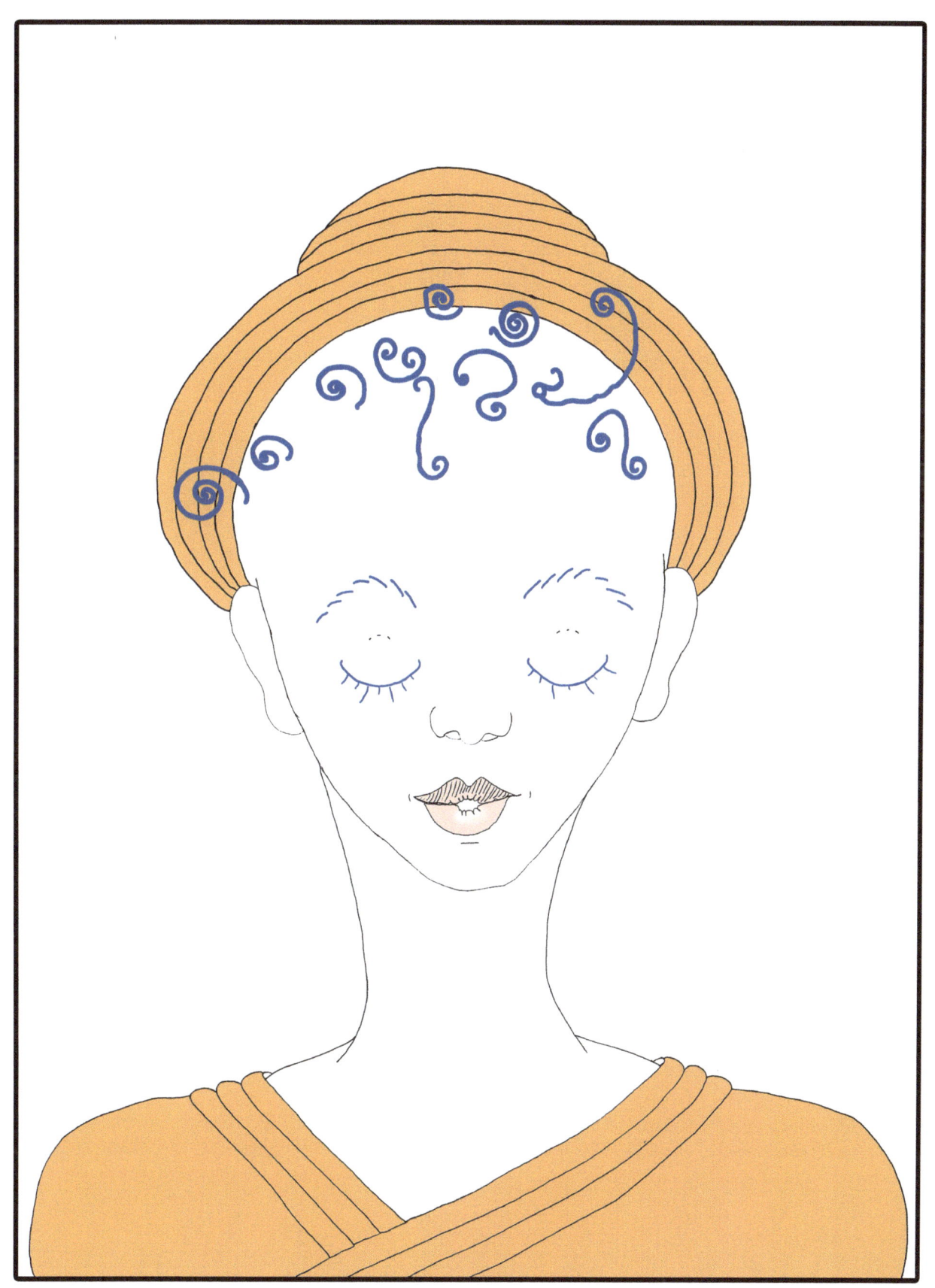

Your thoughts and ideas;
Keep them under control,
Before you lose your heart
And your mind and your soul.

Take a strong rope
Or, even a chain
And try to hold down
That runaway brain!

The End?

www.ingramcontent.com/pod-product-compliance
Lightning Source LLC
Chambersburg PA
CBHW060808290526
45792CB00005BA/1566